THE FIRST GREEN CHRISTMAS

HOW TO MAKE THIS HOLIDAY AN ECOLOGICAL CELEBRATION

BY THE EVERGREEN ALLIANCE

HALO BOOKS
SAN FRANCISCO, CALIFORNIA

It is better to give than to receive

A Green Christmas Gift

for: _____

from: _____

THIS BOOK IS PRINTED ON RECYCLED PAPER
WITH RECYCLED INK.

Published by:

HALO BOOKS
P.O. Box 2529, San Francisco, CA 94126

Copyright © 1990 by Halo Books

Created by The Evergreen Alliance

Cover and Illustrations by Susan Larson

All rights reserved. No part of this book may be reproduced, stored in
a retrieval system, or transmitted in any form or by any means:
electronic, mechanical, photocopying, recording or otherwise, except
for the inclusion of brief quotations in a review, without prior permis-
sion of the copyright owner.

Printed in the United States of America

Library of Congress Catalog Number
90-41498

Library of Congress Cataloging-in-Publication Data
1. Christmas. 2. Human ecology. I. Evergreen Alliance
GT 4985.F53   1991   363.7'057   90-41498
ISBN 0-9622874-9-0

For Ordering Information, write to
HALO BOOKS
P.O. Box 2529
San Francisco, CA 94126
Bulk rate available.

Distributor to the Book Trade: Publishers Group West
Printed by Delta Lithograph Co.

For the adored child this first Christmas.

ACKNOWLEDGEMENTS

*The Evergreen Alliance wishes to
acknowledge the help and support from these people and
organizations, without whom this little book would
still be a distant gleam.*

Susan Larson
Samm Coombs
Dr. Robert West
Hal Larson
Julie Bennett
Robin Dellabough, The Earthworks
Nancy May
Dick McLean
Park Rangers, Jill and Les Allert
Nicky Dahne, National Wildlife Federation
Chinaberry Books
Earthworks Paper Company
Gretchen Hecht
Artype
Gabriella West

TABLE OF CONTENTS

CHRISTMAS 1990:
A TURNING POINT

This little book is a celebration of the first Christmas of the Green Decade. And it has echoes of Christmases past.

In bygone days, Christmas was a time of bonding, of renewal, of reminding ourselves why we're here on this earth. We dropped our guard at Christmastime and allowed ourselves to be more vulnerable, more truly human.

The gifts we gave were from the heart — often made with our hands. We came together, as families, as friends and neighbors. Whatever our individual fortunes, the Holiday Season left us feeling richer, more hopeful.

Then Christmas began to change. "Green" came to represent something more material. We may have given more, but we cared less. A "Cool Yule" with designer trees sprayed pink became the fashion. Until the fallout from "progress" began to tarnish the quality of our lives.

Now, on this first Christmas of the 90's, nature's green is making a comeback. Personal is replacing artificial. The traditional, old-fashioned Christmas is back in style — just in time to uncomplicate our lives and make the Holidays merrier.

The First Green Christmas celebrates this turnaround, offering a houseful of "green" ideas to make your Holidays happier, your environment healthier.

"God Bless us everyone!"
— Tiny Tim

I.
THE MEANING
OF GREEN

Money doesn't grow on Christmas trees.

Once Upon A Time, the word "green" in connection with Christmas brought to mind Nature's greenery — as in *evergreen.* How this got started is reviewed in Section II, *O' Christmas Tree.*

But since the Industrial Revolution turned Christmas into a global merchandising event, *greenbacks* have replaced *evergreens.* Notwithstanding the editorials that admonish us to "take the green out of Christmas," this more material meaning has given us a holiday of a different hue.

Even so, is the commercialization of Christmas really so terrible? After all, it comes but once a year. How can that harm our planet?

Consider the price we pay for this annual consuming frenzy. In addition to the 50 million trees that are cut for Christmas in the U.S., many times that number are turned into wrapping paper and packaging. Our gutters runneth over with December's excess. The mountains of garbage that pile up the next day include tons of plastic, styrofoam and other non-biodegradable, non-recyclable refuse that will be with us for centuries.

All this celebrating consumes an incredible amount of non-renewable energy. This keeps our power plants working overtime, further degrading the environment and depleting our dwindling supply of fossil fuels.

It's a melancholy truth that some 70% of our discretionary purchases are made during November and December—when we are least likely to be discriminating "green consumers"!

The Good News

You can have the merriest of Christmases while reducing the season's negative impact on the environment. It's fun and easy, and you can save greenbacks in the process.

If you were only to keep the oven door closed, use low-energy lights on your tree, and buy cards and wrapping paper made from recycled paper, you would help make the world a better place.

That's one of the advantages of being a populous nation. When a few million people save a few watts, it adds up to millions of kilowatts, and thousands of barrels of foreign oil that don't have to be transported to our power plants.

Of course, there's a lot more you can do to make this first Christmas of the green decade a truly green Christmas. Read on.

The care of the Earth is our most ancient and most worthy and, after all, our most pleasing responsibility. To cherish what remains of it, and to foster its renewal, is our only legitimate hope.
—Wendall Berry
"The Unsettling of America"

II.
O' CHRISTMAS TREE

How to have your Christmas tree and evergreen forests too.

Whatever its size and genus — pine, spruce or fir — the conical evergreen is the centerpiece of Christmas. It fills homes with the fresh scent of winter woods and lights the way for Santa's late night visit. And come Christmas morning, everyone gathers 'round the tree to open the presents piled underneath.

CUTTING DOWN ON CUTTING DOWN

In America's pioneer days, forests were abundant and trees were free for the chopping.

Today, however, we know every green growing thing is an asset to be protected. Some 50 million evergreens fall each year here in the U.S. in the name of Christmas, and an estimated 80 million worldwide are lost to the season.

It's true that more and more of the trees destined for harvesting are planted and grown for that purpose on "Christmas Tree Farms," minimizing the impact on our native forests. So don't feel guilty about cutting the family tree at one of those special-purpose tree farms.

However, you can make a positive contribution to the carbon dioxide cycle, reducing the so-called "greenhouse" gases in the atmosphere, by growing your own. And as long as you're at it, why not grow some more to give as presents two or three years hence.

There is something especially satisfying about fostering a tree — any tree, any time, anywhere. Parenting a *Christmas tree* that will be the center of attention during this sacred time of year is even more pleasurable.

Indeed, if each of us were to leave only a tree to mark our moment on earth, we would be remembered longer and better for it!

You don't need a lot of land, or even a garden. A few pots and lots of TLC will do. A local nursery or garden supply store can tell you how.

Next best to growing your own is buying one already grown. A living Christmas tree is more expensive than a cut tree. But it doesn't take many Christmases before that living tree will start saving you money.

A living tree will never become a torch.
—Andrew Casper
Former Fire Chief, San Francisco, CA

The Top Dozen

What is the ideal live Christmas tree?

Depends on where you live, what you want to spend, size requirements and how much growth you can accommodate in the future.

Also, consider whether you plan to plant it out or keep it in a container, and the kind of trees it will have for neighbors.

On the following pages is a chart of the dozen most popular species used for living Christmas trees.

DOUGLAS FIR	**NOBLE FIR**	**WHITE FIR**
(Pseudotsuga menziesii)	*(Abies procera)*	*(A. concolor)*
Nursery Sizes: 3 to 7 Feet	**Nursery Sizes:** 3 to 6 Feet	**Nursery Sizes:** 1 to 6 Feet
Price: $16 to $50	**Price:** $20 to $60	**Price:** $15 to $90
Container Growth: 1 to 2 Feet Yearly	**Container Growth:** 4 Inches Yearly	**Container Growth:** 1 to 4 Inches Yearly
Best Climates: North East and West, Midwest and Rockies	**Best Climates:** North East and West, Midwest and Rockies	**Best Climates:** Most Anywhere

NORWAY SPRUCE	**DWARF ALBERTA SPRUCE**	**COLORADO BLUE SPRUCE**
(Picea abies)	*(P. glauca 'conica')*	*(P. pungens 'Glauca')*
Nursery Sizes: 3 to 7 Feet	**Nursery Sizes:** 1 to 4 Feet	**Nursery Sizes:** 1 to 6 Feet
Price: $4 to $90	**Price:** $4 to $90	**Price:** $6 to $12
Container Growth: 2 to 12 Inches Yearly	**Container Growth:** 4 Inches Yearly in Youth Slows Later and Never Becomes Tall	**Container Growth:** 1 to 5 Inches Yearly
Best Climates: Most Anywhere Except: South and Deserts	**Best Climates:** Most Anywhere Except: Low and Intermediate Deserts	**Best Climates:** Most Anywhere

SCOTCH PINE	**NORFOLK ISLAND PINE**	**JAPANESE BLACK PINE**
(Pinus sylvestris)	*(Araucaria heterophylla)*	*(P. thubergiana)*
Nursery Sizes: 2 to 8 Feet	**Nursery Sizes:** 1½ to 7 Feet	**Nursery Sizes:** 1½ to 6 Feet
Price: $5 to $75	**Price:** $13 to $90	**Price:** $5 to $75
Container Growth: 1 to 2 Feet Yearly	**Container Growth: Indoors:** 7 Inches Yearly **Outdoors:** 14 Inches Yearly	**Container Growth:** 1½ to 2 Feet Yearly
Best Climates: North East and West, Midwest and Rockies	**Best Climates:** Tropical, Subtropical, Southwest, South, Gulf Coast or as a Houseplant.	**Best Climates:** Most Anywhere

ALEPPO PINE	**MONTEREY PINE**	**MONDELL PINE**
(P. halepensis)	*(P. radiata)*	*(P. eldarica)*
Nursery Sizes: 2 to 6 Feet	**Nursery Sizes:** 2 to 8 Feet	**Nursery Sizes:** 1 to 8 Feet
Price: $4 to $65	**Price:** $12 to $75	**Price:** $6 to $70
Container Growth: Fast—2 to 6 Feet Yearly	**Container Growth:** Fast—2 to 8 Feet Yearly	**Container Growth:** Fast—1 to 8 Feet Yearly
Best Climates: South, Southwest and Low and Intermediate Deserts	**Best Climates:** North, Midwest, East , West in Low Elevations	**Best Climates:** Southwest

TAKE CARE

Don't plan to keep a living tree indoors more than two weeks, three weeks maximum. And don't position it close to any heat sources, including an unshaded south-facing window. Set it in water after spraying with an antitranspirant to help prevent moisture loss.

Heat-generating Christmas tree lights do minimal damage when they come in contact with the needles and this can be minimized with the new "cool" 5W lights being sold this year.

Your living tree arrives in a peat pot or metal can, neither of which is particularly Christmassy. There are a number of can wraps that provide a festive facade while adding to the tree's dignity.

These trees in pots can get heavy. One easy way to move them is on your kid's skateboard.

Give your tree a good soaking before bringing it in. Best to do this a day or two early, so it doesn't create a puddle on the floor.

You should water your tree every three days it is in the house. Idea is to keep the soil moist.

To give your tree time-released watering, try using ice cubes. The tree continues to get water as the cubes melt.

YOUR LIVING TREE LIVES ON

The real beauty of a living Christmas tree is that it stays around all year to provide photo-synthesis, shade, aroma and beauty. It gives you "Christmas every day."

Think carefully about where you want the tree to live until next Christmas: in its container or in the ground. Consult your nursery for advice about your specific tree.

Generally, if it was taken from the ground this Christmas, treat your tree with loving care. Keep it out of high wind locations and give it part shade.

Fertilize in Spring and Summer. Fish emulsion is a good fertilizer, and slow-release chemicals are also recommended.

After two or three years, your tree may become cramped in its pot. Because you don't want it to outgrow your house, you'll need to artfully prune its roots — a subject too detailed for this forum. There are guides to this gentle art at any nursery or library.

RECYCLING CUT TREES

When it comes time to dispose of your cut tree, one option is to take it to a local nursery that has facilities for composting trees. Or, if you have your own compost pile, cut the branches into small pieces; the trunk can be saved for firewood.

Although burning those dry branches and brittle needles in the fireplace creates a roaring fire, however brief, it's not good practice because of the pine tar it distributes in your flu and chimney. Play it safe and recycle the needles and branches as suggested.

WHAT TO DO WITH NON-LIVING TREES

Artificial trees made from plastic and metal pose a different problem. They can't be recycled, and we want to keep them out of our refuse stream. In fact, the whole idea of artificial trees is to keep them for reuse. And when you don't want it any longer, donate it to someone else: young folks starting out; a home for the elderly; a hospice; orphanage. Your dead tree still has a life for someone.

YOUR VERY OWN MEMORIAL CHRISTMAS TREE GROVE

Some families with large lots buy a new living Christmas tree each season. In time, they will have a small forest of trees from Christmases past — a nice way to create a monument to each Christmas.

Living Christmas trees also make the ideal green Christmas gift. Those that are small enough to mail become someone's personal tree, and in time, will grow into a family tree! Many Christmas tree lots and garden centers offer more sizeable specimens for in-person giving.

Knocking on someone's door with a well-garlanded two-foot spruce in your arms will assure you of a warm reception, perhaps a toddy. More about the giving of greenery will be found under the heading, *Gifts That Help.*

Ideas for decorating your Christmas tree are in the next chapter, *Deck The Halls.*

*A living tree is one of
God's greatest gifts: It makes
today more beautiful, and
it affects eternity.*

III.

DECK THE HALLS

*The new fashion in Christmas
decorations is old-fashioned.*

The way we celebrate Christmas says a lot
about our past, as well as our future. This first
Christmas of the "green decade" is an opportunity to
demonstrate our new environmental awareness.
And what better way than by our choice of decorations. These ornamental symbols set the mood and
define the attitude of your household.

EDIBLE ORNAMENTS

If "natural," "homemade," "old-fashioned" and "traditional" describe the feeling you want your decorations to convey, a good place to start is with **popcorn** or **cranberry strings**. Drape these around the tree instead of phony flocking or metallic "ice cycles."

Popcorn and cranberries can also be shaped into ornamental stars and hearts by stringing them on medium gauge wire, bent to the desired shape. Add a bow and hang them from your tree and other appropriate places.

Sweet **candy wreaths** are also easy to make, but be careful to pick a candy that can be strung, and won't go soft and drip chocolate on the carpet.

The best thing about **cookie ornaments** is how easily they disappear after Christmas; no packing necessary. Use a dough that's sturdy: gingerbread or sugar cookie dough. Poke a hole at the tip using a drinking straw. Thread a ribbon through it, tie in a large loop and hang on a bough of your tree.

ORGANIC DECORATIONS

Your garden is probably full of good ideas for Christmas ornaments. Rosettes of pine cones, fallen branches and clumps of berries artfully done up with a beautiful bow are great for the mantlepiece. Include a few red apples, and you have the perfect centerpiece for your Christmas feast.

Clusters of pine cones, red berries and evergreen sprigs at each place-setting echo the centerpiece, but take care: Holly berries are poisonous and should be avoided near food.Toyon or pyracantha berries are perfectly safe.

Make a festive door hanging of a swag of waxy, leathery leaves that are naturally durable — aucuba, boxwood, madrone, Oregon grape, toyon, Southern magnolia — integrated with mossy twigs, citrus and seed pods.

Instead of the traditional evergreen or holly wreath, use corn husks looped through wire to make a natural rustic wreath.

AROMATIC ORNAMENTS

Hang a **pomander ball** dotted with patches of orange rind and cloves for a holiday scent. Or cover a small cardboard ring in glue and dip into a bin of **potpourri**. **Rosemary** sprigs can be fashioned into a fragrant decorative tree that sits on a wreath made of **cinnamon** sticks. Fashion a heart-shaped lace sachet filled with **lavender**.

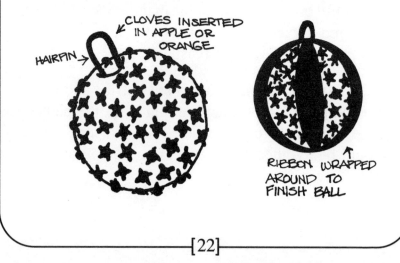

CLOVES INSERTED IN APPLE OR ORANGE

HAIRPIN →

RIBBON WRAPPED AROUND TO FINISH BALL

LET THERE BE LIGHT

Here's a warm welcome to guide guests to your front door: Slip paper-punched luminarias over outdoor light fixtures. Create a Christmas tree design with a paper punch. Ordinary brown paper bags produce a warm glow. Enough light escapes through the punched holes to show your guests to your door.

Another illuminating idea is to collect a bunch of tin cans; fill them full of water and freeze. It will now be easy to punch holes in the shape of fir trees or stars around the sides. Use big nails if you don't have a proper punch. Place a votive candle at the bottom.

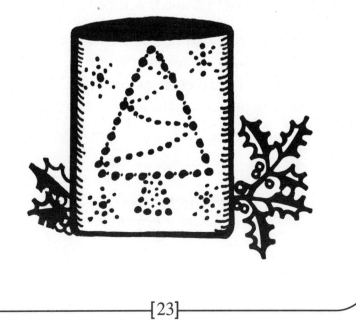

WINDOW PAINTINGS

What child can resist the opportunity to cover the front or bedroom windows with giant cutouts of Christmas graffiti. A fir tree, Santa, reindeer and stars are favorite subjects.

The idea is not to make *better* decorations, but to create *your* decorations. In the process, you'll save a pile of greenbacks and a few trips to the store.

But the best part of doing it yourself is in the doing. Those homemade decorations you keep from year to year will add memories to future Christmases. No store-bought ornament, however exquisite, can offer that.

The loveliest works of man
have Nature's helping hand.

IV.
GIFTS THAT HELP

***This year, instead of taking from
the earth, give to the earth.***

The best Christmas gifts are the "green" kind:
Those that help revitalize our planet.

Most glorious of all is a tree, the ultimate
"Green Christmas" present. What other gift grows
into a monument and does so much good?

In Section II, we noted that the kind of tree to
give or have is a *live* tree — a gift that keeps giving,
a life that keeps growing.

If you plan to send your evergreen gift by mail, packing can prove a bit tricky. Better to depend on a mail order firm like **The Nature Company**. They guarantee the tree will arrive full of life. The

Nature Company recommends three hardy, adaptable species: Black Hills Spruce, Green Ash, Red Maple @ $16 each. One tollfree call to **1-800-227-1114** will save you hours of shopping, gallons of gas and will make the   earth a better place to call home.

Wildflower Seeds carry the spirit of Christmas into Spring. You can buy packets of mixes (featuring American and European plants that naturalize most readily) wherever you find seed racks. You can also order by mail from these wildflower specialists:
Moon Mountain Wildflowers, Box 34, Morro Bay, CA 93442.
Native Plants, Inc., Box 177, Lehi, Utah 84043.
Larner Seeds, Box 407,Bolinas, CA 94924.
Wildflower Seed Co., Box 406, St. Helena, CA 94574.
Southwestern Native Seeds, Box 5053, Tucson, AZ 85703.

Also in the flora category of gift, consider this easy-to-make **Gift terrarium**.

🧺 SOIL

🪨 CHARCOAL

⬤ GRAVEL

Select any wide-mouth, attractively-shaped clear jar (a ½-gallon juice jar is fine) with a lid. Add 1 to 2 inches (depending on jar's size) of pea gravel, about an inch of charcoal, and 1 to 2 inches of potting soil. Set down inside one or more houseplants. Ferns are an ideal choice. Add more potting soil to the top of the root ball. Lightly moisten soil and close lid. Display it in a well-lighted area out of dirext sunlight. More water is usually not needed; the terrarium transpires, creating its own moisture.

Beyond The Poinsettia: Other Christmassy plants that make ideal Holiday Calling Cards and office gifts: **Kalanchoe**, **Freesia**, **Miniature Roses**, **Narcissus**, **Cyclamen**, **Chrysanthemum** and **Christmas cactus**.

Born-Again Flower Pots: If you are making a gift of plants or flowers, make use of old plastic bottles (quart, $1/2$-gallon or gallon size) by cutting off the upper portion and scalloping the top edge. To decorate, tie a ribbon around the base and/or use decals and felt-tip markers.

Flea-Free Fido: If you have a dog and live near any eucalyptus trees, gather the bell-shaped pods you'll find around the roots. With a needle threaded with dental floss, string them through the soft centers and slip the necklace around your dog's neck. People like the nice tangy smell, but fleas can't stand it.

GIVE SOMETHING OF YOURSELF

The following do-it-yourself ideas cost little or nothing, can be done quickly, and don't require a lot of tools or talent.

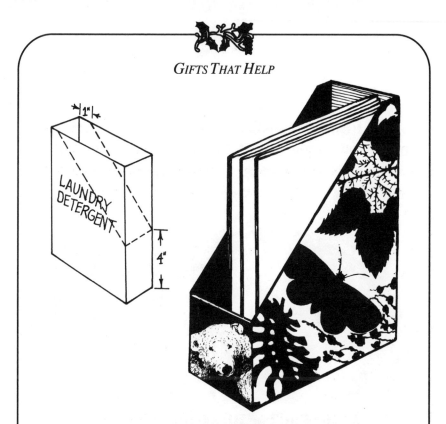

Soapbox Magazine Holder: Save all those giant-size (49-oz.) laundry detergent boxes. With an X-acto knife or scissors, cut from the top down each side at an angle to a point approximately 4" from the bottom. If the person it's intended for saves National Geographic Magazines, glue a photo collage of exotic, faraway places on the outside. If the holder is intended for the readers of a weekly news magazine, cut out "1991" and combine with current affairs pictures. If the subject is business, choose business-like pictures. It's a thoughtful gift and a practical way to put old cardboard to good use.

Edible Christmas Cards: Bake a greeting card to show you care. Make a giant version of your favorite cookie, put a personal greeting on with icing, and watch your friends eat it up.

A Gift For The Birds: Spread sugarless peanut butter on pine cones and roll in wild birdseed. Like kids, birds love peanut butter, and it provides protein and oils for healthy feathers and bodies. Fasten the cones to the branches of a tree, using floral wire.

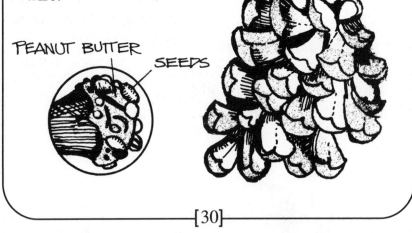

Another gift for our fine-feathered friends is a simple bird-feeder made from a half-gallon milk carton. Cut a "window" from the side of the carton and place a dowel or small tree branch from side-to-side beneath the window with the ends poking through holes on either side. Fill the bottom with bird seed and hang from the top, using a sturdy waxed line like fishing line or cat gut leader material.

Etcetera: Hot mitts, pot holders, knitted stocking caps, teapot cozies, aprons, log carriers, finger puppets, grocery tote bags (to avoid plastic or paper throwaways) are among the many ideas for quick'n'easy do-it-yourself gifts.

GIVE WARMTH

A major gift for a special person is a **goose-down comforter**. It'll save a modest fortune in heating bills.

Or a **hot water bottle** or **warm wooly pajamas**.

Or an **automatic thermostat** that turns the heat down at night, up in the morning.

MORE ENVIRONMENTAL GIFTS

Enrollment in a **diaper service** is a most welcome gift for new parents.

A **water-saving attachment for the toilet or shower** is another way to give to the earth while you give to your friend.

A **nozzle that shuts the water off at the working end of a hose**

is a welcome and water-saving gift for the dedicated car-washer.

A **reusable mesh shopping bag** eliminates the need for non-biodegradable plastic or tree-consuming paper bags.

Gifts From The Sun

Some solar-powered gifts to brighten lives and save energy:

Solar battery chargers and rechargeable batteries. **Sunwatt Corporation**, P.O. Box 751, Addison, ME 04606. Phone (207) 497-2204.

A **solar garden lamp** for patios and walkways. Provides five hours of night light. **Chronar Sunenergy**, P.O. Box 177, Princeton, NJ 08542. Phone (207) 497-2204.

A **solar-powered radio and earphones**. Gives you four hours of play for each three hours in the sun. **Solar Electric Engineering**, 175 Cascade Court, Rohnert Park, CA 94928. Phone (707) 586-1987.

SOLAR KIDS' STUFF

A **4-in-1 Solar Construction Kit** for youngsters to make solar-powered airplanes, helicopters and windmills. Also a safari hat, tea jar, flashlight—even a solar-powered speedboat. **Jade Mountain**, P.O. Box 4616, Boulder, CO 80306. Phone (303) 449-6601.

Project Books show kids how to make such fascinating things as solar ovens, site-finders and sundials. The books also have ideas on how to use these creations.

Sun Prints demonstrate the artistic side of solar energy. When the light-sensitive paper is exposed to the sun, a positive image appears where objects have touched the paper. Image changes to negative when developed in tap water.

GIFTS FROM THE "GREEN LIBRARY":

From our planet's point of view, the most helpful gift around this year is a $4.95 book titled **50 Simple Things You Can Do To Save The Earth**. Like the book you're holding, it's printed on recycled paper. (*Earth Works Press*)

Other gift titles on the Green Bookshelf:

Blueprint For A Green Planet by John Seymour and Herbert Girardet (*Prentice Hall*) $14.95

Let It Rot! Home Gardener's Guide To Composting, by Stu Campbell (*Garden Way Publishing*), $5.95

Energy Conservation: A Campus Guidebook, by Kevin O'Brien and David Corn (*Center For Study of Responsive Law*), $5.

Your Affordable Solar Home, by Dan Habshmam (*Sierra Club Books/Random House*), $7.95

The Natural Garden, by Ken Druse (*Crown Publishers*), $35.

Jacques Cousteau's Amazon Journey, by Jacques-Yves Cousteau and Mose Richards (*Henry M. Abrams*), $39.95

For children and young adults:

Chadwich the Crab, by Priscilla Cummings (*Tidewater Publications*), $5.95

Teenage Survival Manual, by Samm Coombs (*Discovery Books*), $9.95

The Planet of Trash, An Environmental Fable, by George Poppel (*National Press*), $9.95

The Kids' Nature Book, *Williamson Publishing*, provides a day-by-day guide, listing 365 things kids can do for their planet.

HELP THE HELPFUL

Here's a list of worthwhile non-profit organizations which are always strapped for the means to do good. And your gift is tax deductible. These groups will send a nice acknowledgement to whomever you name.

Friends of the Urban Forest is dedicated to the proposition that cities need trees, too. The Wilderness Society, 116 New Montgomery,# 526, San Francisco, CA 94105. (415) 541-9144.

The Audubon Society is at the forefront of every fight to save birds' habitat. National Audubon Society, 645 Pennsylvania Ave., SE, Washington, D.C. 20003.

Sierra Club, 730 Polk St., San Francisco, CA 94109; (415) 776-2211, promotes conservation of the natural environment. Make a gift of a $33 membership (includes subscription to the monthly magazine *Sierra*, which is worth the price of admission).

Earth Island Institute, 300 Broadway, Ste. 28, San Francisco, CA 94133; (415) 788-3666, Supports international projects protecting and restoring the environment. A $25 membership includes the quarterly *Earth Island Journal*.

The Nature Conservancy, 1815 N. Lynn St., Arlington, VA 22209; (703) 841-5300, acts to preserve ecosystems and the rare species they shelter. The $15 annual membership gives you a bimonthly magazine, *The Nature Conservancy Magazine.*

The Wilderness Society, 1400 Eye St., NW, Washington, DC 20005; (202) 842-3400, protects wildlands, wildlife, forests, parks, rivers and shorelines. First year membership is $15. Includes a bimonthly newsletter, *The Wildlifer*.

Friends of the Earth, 530 7th St. SE, Washington, DC 20003; (202) 544-2600, promotes the conservation, protection and rational use of the earth and its land-based and oceanic resources. Memberships run $25 ($15 for students, senior citizens), and include the monthly magazine, *No Man Apart*.

World Wildlife Fund, (416) 923-8173, saves our dwindling rainforests. For $25 you can save an acre. Use Mastercard, Visa, check or money order. You'll receive a packet with decal and certificate identifying the recipient as a Guardian of the Amazon.

Rainforest Action Network, 430 E. University, Ann Arbor, MI 48109; (313) 764-2147, focuses on the preservation, protection and rational use of rain forests. $10 donation includes its newsletter, *Tropical Echoes*, published every six weeks.

Greenpeace, 1436 U St. NW, Washington, DC 20009; (202) 462-1177, has concentrated its efforts on halting the wanton killing of marine mammals and other endangered creatures, toxic waste reduction and nuclear disarmament. The $20 annual membership provides the bimonthly *Greenpeace* magazine.

Greenhouse Crisis Foundation, 1130 17th St. NW, Ste 630, Washington, DC 20036; (202) 466-2823, is dedicated to creating a global awareness of the greenhouse crisis.

Environmental Defense Fund, 257 Park Ave. S, New York, NY 10010; (212) 505-2100, is concerned with water pollution, pesticides, wildlife preservation, wetlands protection, rain forests, toxic rain, the ozone layer, toxic chemicals and waste. The $20 annual membership includes the quarterly *EDF Newsletter*.

STOCKING STUFFERS

Subscription to outdoor magazines, such as: **Sunset**, **National Geographic**, **E The Environmental Magazine**, **Audubon** for Adults. **The National Wildlife Federation** offers magazines for kids: **Your Own Backyard** and **Ranger Rick**.

Tickets to a Local Nature Museum.

A Pocket-Sized Field Guide. These are guides that identify birds, trees, flowers, fish, animals. Educational and fun.

Biodegradable Soaps and Shampoos. You'll find 'em at your local Health Food Store.

Free Booklets and Reprints from the **U.S. Geological Survey**. A catalog listing material on such subjects as volcanoes and earthquakes. Write Distribution Branch, USGS, P.O. Box 25286, Federal Center, Denver, CO 80225.

Bicycling and Hiking Path Maps in your community.

Gifts from Environmental Catalogs. Excellent gifts can be found in catalogs from: **World Wildlife Fund, Save Our Ecosystems, Inc., Sierra Club, National Wildlife Federation, Rainforest Action Network, The Nature Conservancy, Environmental Action, National Audubon Society, The Cousteau Society, Greenpeace**, and **Center for Marine Conservation.**

GIVE A GARDEN

Simply assemble all the elements needed for one garden project: For a salad garden, include gloves, soil, lettuce plants or seeds in a shallow pot. A rose garden should include a deep pot, soil, pruning shears and packaged roses. An herb garden is another thoughtful possibility.

GIVE A NATURE WALK

Here's a do-it-yourself gift you don't have to make: A hike. The giver leads the way to some special place you want to share with one or more friends, relatives, neighbors. If you don't live near woods or shore, plan an urban trek.

GIFTS TO AVOID

Some pets are wonderful gifts: dogs, cats, rabbits. Some should never be taken from their native environment: **parrots, snakes, turtles and other exotic creatures**. They contribute to the health of the environment in their natural habitat, and they generally suffer elsewhere.

Also avoid:

✔ Those little boxes, carvings and bowls made of **tropical hardwoods** such as mahogany, teak, rosewood or satinwood.

✔ **Ivory**. Scrimshaw, carvings, sculpture, boxes, jewelry — any kind of ivory.

✔ **Throwaways**. Avoid single-use toothbrushes, razors, cameras, clothing. They add to the problem.

✔ **Electrical Jimcracks.** Better to use energy where it's really needed. Not on pocket fans, delinters, noisemakers, foot warmers and electric whoopee cushions.

✔ **Plants.** Some plants such as cycads, orchids, and cacti face extinction because they have been smuggled from their native land.

✔ **Furs.** Seals and other marine mammals, polar bear, jaguar, tiger cat, snow leopard, jaguar, ocelot, margay, tiger.

✔ **Plastic City.** Eschew trinkets, keyholders, toys, novelties made from non-renewable petroleum.

Put the Earth on your shopping list this Christmas

V.
WRAPPING IT UP

Wherein we reveal more than one way to wrap your Christmas gifts

It's anyone's guess how many trees are sacrificed each year to make paper for Christmas gift wrapping. Much of it isn't paper at all, but takes the form of foil or mylar, which isn't biodegradable and hence can't be recycled.

A lot of the paper has a waxed or glazed finish, creating the same problem. (The gloss is created by a coating that gums up recycling machinery.) So

anything you can do to reduce reliance on those specialty papers will go a long way toward reducing the waste disposal problem that comes in the wake of Christmas.

A simple solution is to purchase Christmas cards and wrapping material made from recycled paper. That won't cost the earth another tree, and this material can be recycled again. This year, there should be a large selection of recycled giftwrap on the market. If you can't find any in your area, you can order by mail.

One of the many paper product companies specializing in gift wrap and greeting cards made from recycled paper is **Earth Care Paper Company**. Products are distributed by **Co-Op America**, 10 Farrell Street, South Burlington, VT 05403 (802) 658-5507. Ask for their $1 catalog and the names and addresses of retailers in your area.

You can always fill your gift list with presents that require no wrapping. (In the previous chapter, we mentioned a number of possibilities — such as giving to good causes that send an acknowledgement of your gift to the recipient on recycled paper.)

RECYCLED WRAPPINGS

Yet another way to wrap your gifts without adding to the earth's disposal dilemma is to create colorful wrappings from material you already have lying around.

This offers the additional benefit of putting something of yourself

into the wrap. It's creative, fun, and ecologically smart.

Some easy-to-do suggestions:

- Paste old Christmas cards on old shopping bags. Bright, Christmassy and happy.

- Use old maps or posters.

- Wrap your gifts to children in old colored comic pages.

- Personalize the wrapping by using selected magazine pages.

- Decorate brown paper grocery bags with a rubber stamp of your favorite Christmas design, using red and green ink pads, or use crayons and water colors.

- Beautify old butcher or kraft paper with homemade stamps fashioned from kitchen

sponges cut into the shape of a Christmas tree, star, or other holiday symbol—or use half slices of citrus fruit dipped in acrylic paint.

- Use leftover wallpaper

- Reuse wrappings from gifts you receive.

- Wrap with the pages of large 1990 calendars

PAPER ALTERNATIVES

There's no rule that says gifts must be wrapped in paper. This Christmas, make use of other material for inventive ecological alternatives.

- Wrap in handkerchiefs or bandanas; the wrapping itself is a gift.

- Send the gift in a Christmas stocking.

- Put it in a pillow case.

- Use a cookie jar, coffee can, mug, piñata.

- Decorate a flower pot and put the gift inside.

- Put breakables in old egg cartons.

- Give edibles in a breadbox or lunchbox.

- Wrap the gift in Christmas fabric, "Hobo style," and pin shut with a corsage.

- Send it in a servicable canvas tote bag, a wrapper that becomes a traveling companion.

- Put the gift in a handy bucket.

AN EDIBLE CONTAINER

Give Christmas cookies in a bowl made of leftover cookie dough. Gingerbread bowls are big winners.

AND TIE IT UP...

- Recycle old bows and ribbons.
- If the gift is for a dog, tie it with a leash.
- Use cotton yarn or twine or other bio-degradable material instead of plastic ribbons.
- Tie it with decorative shoe laces.
- Use hair ribbons.

AND TAG IT.

A picture, as we've heard, is worth a bunch of words. You can create a unique gift tag using a **photo** of the recipient.

Or if it's someone you haven't seen for some time, use both your picture and the receiver's. It'll close the gap of years and induce a warm rememberance.

Other tag ideas:
- Old Christmas cards
- Origami folded papers in Christmas shapes.
- Snowflakes made from cut-out paper.

HOW TO PAD THE PACKAGE...

You can prevent the contents of any package from being damaged in transit without resorting to foam padding or plastic bubble wrap. The solution is **popcorn** (without salt and butter!).

HOW WE PAY FOR PAPER

Manufacturing wrapping paper "costs" more than trees. To produce one ton of paper requires 261 pounds of lime, 360 pounds of salt cake, 76 pounds of soda ash, 3688 pounds of wood, 24,000 gallons of water, 28,000,000 BTUs of energy! And the manufacturing process produces 176 pounds of solid wastes, 84 pounds of air pollutants, 36 pounds of water pollutants!

Now for the good news: Recycling paper instead of using virgin materials reduces pollutants by 50%, reduces energy use by 70%, reduces water use by 60%. It pays to recycle paper, and to use paper made from recycled paper!

Woodman, spare that tree!
Touch not a single bough!
In my youth it sheltered me,
And I'll protect it now.
—George Morris

VI.
CELEBRATING AT WORK

Christmas provides employers with countless opportunities to lend the environment a helping hand.

It's not unusual to spend two-thirds of our waking hours at work. So the workplace provides special opportunities to upgrade the environment. The office Christmas party is a good place to start.

THE OFFICE PARTY

Here are a few constructive tips for the party planner(s):

✔ **Get the right tree.** Section III outlined the whys and hows of having a living tree, and Section IV offered suggestions for decorating. These activities can be enjoyable *communal* functions at the office or workplace.

And before adjourning for the holidays, hold an office drawing to award the tree to the winning employee.

✔ **Celebrant's carpool.** Especially if alcohol is served at the party, it makes good sense to rent a bus, van, or limousine service to transport people home or to suburban transit stations. Short of that, arrangements should be made for a buddy system to see revelers home safely.

✔ **Rent non-disposable dinner service**. Instead of adding to the world's woes with plastic and styrofoam, rent glasses, plates, utensils and cloth napkins. If you must have disposable material, make it paper.

✔ **Buy in bulk.** Get large economy items to cut down on packaging and travel. Get giant bags of popcorn and chips, kegs of beer, large jugs of soft drinks and wine. Check with restaurant supply houses.

✔ **Buy produce loose.** Get your carrots, oranges, apples, celery, broccoli in bulk — not in small plastic bags.

✔ **Decorate with living beauty.** Order live poinsettias or other plants that can be taken home after the festivities. Other decorating thoughts:

- Use natural greens and pine cones.
- Use easy-to-recycle paper.
- Use timers on lights to conserve energy.
- Avoid using non-recyclable tinsel and foil.

✔ **Eat low on the food chain.** Eschew environmentally costly beef, veal and pork. Go for fruits, fish, poultry, vegetables, grains, nuts. Both the earth and party-goers will be ahead.

Business Gifts

Many companies are beginning to make environmental donations in their employees' and customers' names. Section III lists a number of green gift ideas, and the section following this will offer further outreach suggestions.

Another thought for employee giving is a living Christmas tree. If the number of employees would require a small forest of such trees, consider giving seedlings.

The Tree People, 12601 Mulholland Drive, Beverly Hills, can provide complete starter kits.

Co-worker Gifts

If you give gifts to co-workers, consider these low-cost ecologically sound ideas:

✔ **A living houseplant** for their office work-space: helps clean the air and brighten the area.

✔ **A permanent ceramic coffee cup** to replace disposable and unrecyclable styrofoam.

✔ **A calendar, tee shirt, poster or supply of stationery** from an environmental organization that gives part of the proceeds to planting trees, or to saving rainforests or endangered species.

Company Cards

If your company sends out Christmas cards, consider printing them on recycled paper — or buy pre-printed cards from greeting card companies that print on recycled paper.

Another way to help is to purchase Christmas cards from UNICEF or an environmental organization.

OFFICE RESOLUTIONS

Consider ending the holiday season on an "up" note by holding a staff meeting to make environmental resolutions for the New Year.

- Replace incandescent lights with the new screw-in florescent bulbs.
- Lower the thermostat a couple of degrees.

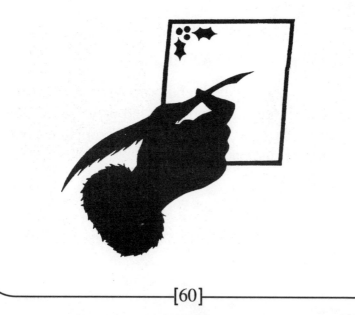

- Institionalize car pooling.
- Establish staggered working hours.
- Get a copier that copies both sides.
- Recycle bottles, cans, paper and cardboard.
- Remove plastic and polystyrene from the cafeteria.
- Print all business forms on recycled paper
- Switch from white paper towels to brown.

One of the most important things to bear in mind when planning your office festivities — or any holiday celebration — is this:

*You don't have to harm the earth
to have a good time.*

VII.
CHRISTMAS IN
THE COMMUNITY

*How your school, church, club,
fraternal organization, youth group, professional
society and other affinity organizations can serve
the environment while celebrating the Holidays.*

Americans are great joiners. Most of us are members of more than a few organizations, and most all these groups acknowledge Christmas with some kind of a get-together.

In this first Christmas of the 90's, we can convert those events into important ways to serve the environment.

COMMUNITY CHRISTMAS PROJECTS

✔ The Audubon Society conducts an annual, **nationwide bird count** between December 18 and January 1, and they need all the volunteer "counters" they can get. Come to them as a group. You don't have to be an accomplished "bird watcher" to help.

✔ **Christmas caroling** is a happy way for your organization to raise money for some good local environmental cause, such as a tree-planting or creek-cleaning project. You'll be more successful in high traffic locations: shopping centers, parks, lobbies of major office buildings, etc. Go where the shoppers are.

✔ Garden clubs and horticultural societies might form an advisory panel to provide **advice/information to local gardeners**.

✔ **Clean-up crews** are always needed to keep-up parks, schools and other public facilities. Your group could adopt a particularly forlorn site and turn it into a garden spot that would be maintained throughout the year. Or sponsor a one -time clean-up effort. There are a number of organizations that will advise you and provide seedlings:

✔ **Trees For Life** (316) 263-7294 runs the "Grow-A-Tree" program, encouraging children to plant trees. It also distributes packets of material, seeds and instructions.

✔ **America The Beautiful Fund** (202)638-1649 provides technical support, small seed grants and free seeds.

✔ **Global Releaf** (202) 667-3300 helps find suitable sites.

✔ **National Arbor Day Foundation** (402) 474-5655 is a source for blue spruce seedlings.

A WAY OF LIFE

Trees breathe life into our planet. They cool our cities. Prevent erosion. Reduce energy needs. Trees are the best defense against a warming planet; they combat the greenhouse effect by absorbing the offending CO_2. The average tree eliminates between 26 and 487 pounds of carbon dioxide every year. An acre of trees will offset the emissions produced by a car traveling 26,000 miles. So you can see — we need all the trees we can get.

CO-OP GARDEN

Another worthwhile project your organization can undertake is a cooperative garden. If your community doesn't set aside land for it, your group could consider buying and donating appropriate space.

Let anyone who's willing to do the work grow his own food. Only minimum administration is required — and the good that it does is very real.

If you have questions about how to get started, call the **American Community Gardening Association**, (213) 744-4341.

ONGOING PROGRAMS
YOUR GROUP CAN JOIN

Some of the worthy environmental programs your organization may wish to work with:

✔ **Center for Environmental Information**, 99 Court St., Rochester, NY 14604. (716) 546-3796, keeps a large library, sets up conferences and seminars and publishes useful ecological information.

✔ **Adopt-A-Stream Foundation**, P.O. Box 5558, Everett, WA 98201. (206) 388-3313, invites your organization to "adopt" a stream. Your group provides for the care of the stream. Write for information on getting started.

✔ **Children of the Green Earth**, P.O. Box 95219, Seattle, WA 98145. (206) 781-0852, helps young people plant and look after forests and trees. They'll show your organization how to become active in your area.

✔ **Citizen's Clearinghouse for Hazardous Waste**, P.O. Box 3541, Arlington, VA 22216. (703) 276-7070, works with some 6,000 community groups for environmental sanity.

✔ **American Forestry Association**, P.O. Box 2000, Washington, DC 20013. (202) 667-3300, works to improve the health of our trees and forests. Also strives to increase awareness of the values of tree planting and conservation.

RECYCLING HELP

Some useful reading material about community recycling projects:

✔ **Planning for Community Recycling: A Citizen's Guide to Resources**. Free. Environmental Action, 1525 New Hampshire Ave. NW, Washington, DC 20036. (202) 745-4870.

✔ **Coming Full Circle: Successful Recycling Today**. $20. The Environmental Defense Fund EDF, Park Ave. S., New York, NY 10010. (212) 505-2100.

✔ **Greenpeace Action Community Recycling Start-up Kit**. Greenpeace Action, 1436 U. St. NW, Washington, DC 20009. (202) 462-1177.

ORGANIZE A RECYCLING DAY

You'll be primarily interested in bottles, cans and paper. But other materials are now being recycled too. Steps to set up the drive:

✔ **Plan.** Assign specific duties and areas. Where, when, how the collection will be made.

✔ **Work with a recycling center.** Be sensitive to their time demands and peak hours.

✔ **Move fast.** Material to be recycled shouldn't lie around. Collections should be prompt and efficient.

✔ **Use the proceeds for a good ecological cause:** starting gardens, planting trees, recycling education, community clean-up, etc.

Whatever your group does to make the earth cleaner and greener as a part of Holiday outreach is a gift to everyone who does or will inhabit the planet.

*All things work together for good
to them that love God.*
—Romans VIII 28

VIII.
THE MORE THE MERRIER

***How to throw a party without giving Mother
Earth a headache.***

The Holiday Season is for get-togethers of all
kinds: Neighborhood parties, office parties,
children's parties, parties by clubs, churches and
other groups. But most of all, Christmas is for
families.

With a little care and concern these good times
won't give the environment a bad time.

FOOD COMES FIRST

Let's begin by ending our love affair with meat. Consider:

- Producing meat uses 10 times the water used to produce the equivalent energy in grain.

- More than 85% of the U.S. Agricultural area is used to grow meat.

Cutting down on meat consumption saves energy, land, and other vital resources. Also, you're better off eating less meat.

Why not try an Olde World favorite—Christmas goose? Or America's traditional Holiday bird, a plump Tom Turkey. Nowhere is it written you can't serve stuffed salmon or other fish. With plenty of grains, fruits, and vegetables.

Bowls of tropical fruits from Brazil are not only great party food. Serving them provides a living for people in the rain forest — without putting a torch to it.

When planning party menus, think of dishes that require little or no energy to prepare:

- Cheese and vegetable dips
- Fruits, nuts, vegetables
- Cheese balls, crackers, popcorn
- No-Bake recipes like this:

Fruit-Nut Party Mix

4 cups tiny pretzels
1 cup dried tart cherries
1 cup salted mixed nuts
1 cup banana chips
Mix and store in airtight container until ready to serve. Makes 7 cups

- Edible serving containers: A hollowed-out bread loaf for dip or cheese; a pumpkin for soup; red pepper for herbs.

SHOP SMART

- Use cloth instead of napkins and towels

- Rent or borrow infrequently used items: Punch bowls, chafing dishes, etc.

- Support the small farmer: shop at Farmers' Markets when possible.

- Buy eggs in cardboard containers instead of styrofoam.

- Go for the large economy sizes for things that won't spoil: rice, soap, sugar, grains, nuts, dried fruits, pet food. You'll save time, gasoline, money — and reduce garbage.

- Buy biodegradable soaps.

- Brings your own tote bag, or cardboard boxes to haul home your purchases.

- And remember: no plastic containers/bags, no aerosol sprays, no non-returnable bottles.

AFTER THE PARTY

Some ecological suggestions for the cleanup crew:

- Recycle aluminum cans.
- Rinse and reuse aluminum foil.
- Wash and reuse glass jars.
- Stick to biodegradable packages.
- Reuse cardboard boxes.
- Recycle magazines and papers.
- Reuse gift paper.
- Use garbage cans, not bags.

LITTLE THINGS MEAN A LOT

It's easy to ignore all these dos and don'ts, calling them mere trifles. A couple of cans, one bottle, a plastic bag. But when millions mind the trifles, the effect is tremendous!

But when I undress me
Each night, upon my knees
Will ask the Lord to bless me
With apple pie and cheese.
                    —Eugene Ford

IX.

KITCHEN CONSERVATION

Tips on saving time, money and energy preparing the Christmas feast.

Kitchens are busy places during the Holidays. So many of the gifts and decorations mentioned earlier are made here. Long before it's time to prepare Christmas Dinner, a stream of friends and relatives comes dropping in, most of them gravitating to the kitchen.

No wonder your December gas and electric bill always is a shocker. Your range is working overtime. The oven's always occupied. The

refrigerator door is seldom closed. The tap runs hot day and night. And the kitchen's lights are among the last to be shut off.

First, make sure your appliances are functioning efficiently. **Test the thermostat in your oven. Check the reflectors under your stove-top burners.** One-third of the energy used for stovetop cooking is wasted because reflectors don't reflect! Make sure yours are bright and shiny. If they won't shine, replace. Or cover with foil shaped to fit. You'll be money ahead.

And make every effort to use the right size pots and pans. The bigger the container, the more energy is used to head the contents. Flat-bottoms are more efficient for electric and smooth cook-tops.

Check the oven door seal. Clean, and if you find any tears or gaps, repair or replace. If you have a gas oven, the pilot light should be a blue, cone-shaped flame. If it's yellow or a jumpy blue, you're wasting gas. Ask your power company to make adjustments.

By using ceramic baking dishes you can lower oven temperatures 25%.

Dust the condenser coils behind or under your refrigerators and check the door seal. This is the most energy-hungry appliance in the kitchen. If your temperature is set below 40°, redial for dollars! (Freezers should be set between 0° and 5°.)

Letting warm leftovers cool before refrigerating is a simple and effective energy-saving habit.

Whatever you do, don't cook with the oven door open. There is no more wasteful practice! And resist peeking. Every time you open the oven door, you waste 25° to 50°, or more.

Don't overdo the pre-heating. 10 minutes is plenty. And remember, pre-heating is unnecessary for broiling.

If you own a microwave oven, use it whenever possible. It uses about 50% less energy than your stove's oven. (If you don't own a microwave, put that on the top of your Christmas Wish List.)

If a lot of water goes down the drain waiting for the sink tap to run hot, keep a jug handy to catch

it. If you don't use it to drink or cook with, you can use this supply for watering plants.

Kitchen lights burn late and long during winter, especially around the Holidays. By substituting the new screw-in compact flourescent bulbs for incandescent, you'll use 75% less energy. For instant ignition and to eliminate flickering and buzzing, obtain the new electronic ballast model. Those new fluorescent lights also keep a half-ton of CO_2 out of the atmosphere over the life of the bulb (which is 10 times longer than incandescent!).

None of these precautions and practices will necessarily make you a better cook. But the energy saved leaves a good taste in everyone's mouth.

*Tis an ill cook that cannot
lick his own fingers.*
— William Shakespheare

X.

HAPPY NEW YEAR!

Making 1991 cleaner and greener.

After the turkey has been picked clean and sits in a pot brewing a wonderful broth; after the day-glo neckties and outsized socks have been exchanged and some semblance of order has been restored to your household — there's a New Year to face.

A happy, healthy New Year, as well as a prosperous one, depends very much on the quality of the environment: locally, regionally, globally.

The environmental conditions that greet us on January 1, 1991 will have been determined by the

actions or inaction of the nine billion humans who have inhabited this planet to date, yourself included.

So what can one person like yourself do in one year to undo the damage done over thousands of years by billions of people? *Plenty*.

> *Nobody made a greater mistake*
> *than he who did nothing because*
> *he could only do a little.*
> —Edmund Burke

Most environmental damage has been wrought in the last 150 years of man's reign. The effects are correctible in even a shorter time frame. Rivers and streams flowing thick with chemical wastes and effluent can be made to run pure again in less than a decade.

England's Thames River, for example, went from being a cesspool to a Salmon-run river in less than 10 years. The soot and grime that once coated

city buildings in many coal-producing regions is now a thing of the past.

We can clear up the air quality in places like the Los Angeles basin, stop acid rain from denuding Eastern forests and prevent any further degrading of the protective ozone layer before the end of this decade — if we are willing to take the trouble and spend the money. The technology is waiting for the will!

There is, of course, one more important thing *you* can do for the earth as we round out this first year of the green decade.

You can make — and persuade your family and friends to make — resolutions to make the world better for the next generation and all generations to come.

NEW YEAR'S RESOLUTIONS

- Plant at least one tree.
- Use only cloth cleaning towels.
- Turn off the shower while you soap.
- Install water-saving devices in your toilet and shower.
- Walk or bicycle at least one car errand weekly.
- Use re-usable cloth bags to shop.
- Get a permanent coffee cup for the job.
- Use biodegradable laundry soap, not detergents.
- Turn down the thermostat at night.
- Recycle your bottles, cans, papers.
- Buy recycled products (those with a Green Seal).
- Think— really think— about the future of our planet.

To see a World in a Grain of Sand,
And a Heaven in a Wild Flower,
Hold Infinity in the palm of your hand,
And Eternity in an hour.
—William Blake

THE LAST WORD

There is one final thing you can do for yourself and the planet you live on.

Share your knowledge! Let others know how they can make their Christmas an ecological celebration.

Christmas, 1990, is the first Green Christmas. A beginning — an important beginning. But only the first.

It's important that you share with your friends, co-workers, neighbors. And if they, too, share the information, Christmas can become a joyous symbol for the greening of the earth.

And if you have ideas, thoughts, or questions about *The* First Green Christmas, please write. We'll see that others get the word.

Write us at:
HALO BOOKS
P.O. BOX 2529
SAN FRANCISCO,
CA 94126